ON THE WATER

by Jason Page

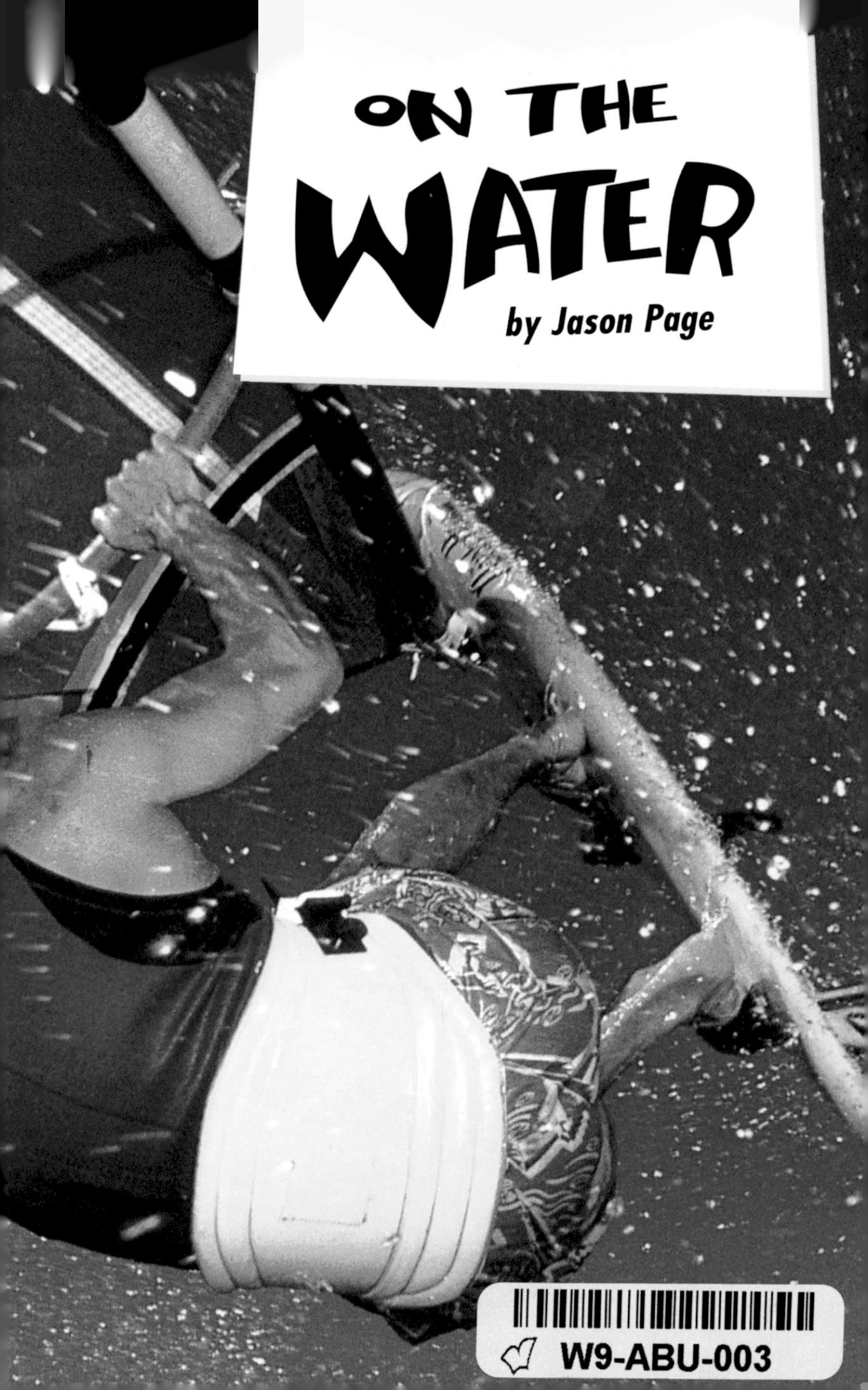

WATER SPORTS

Grab your life jacket and prepare to set sail as competitors take to the water in the Olympic sailing, rowing, and canoeing events!

CANCELED!

Sailing and rowing events were supposed to have been included in the very first modern Olympics, in 1896. But the weather was so bad that the organizers had to cancel the competitions. As a result, both sports had to wait until 1900 to make their Olympic debuts.

SOMETHING OLD

People have been using boats to race on water for thousands of years. One of the earliest examples we know about dates back to 2,500 B. C., when the ancient Egyptians held rowing races on the Nile River.

SUPER STATS

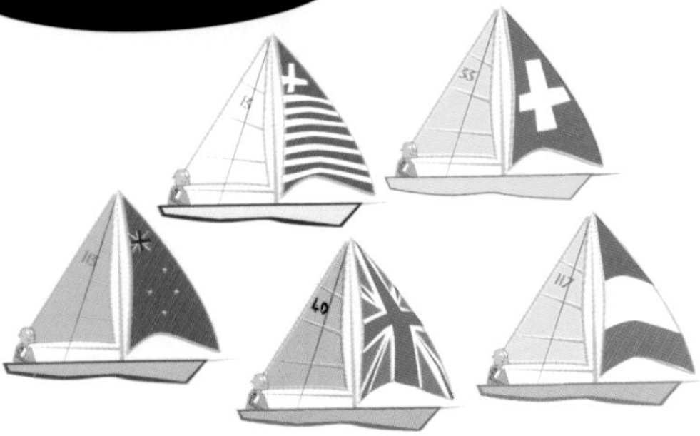

Five countries have attended every single Olympic Games since the competition began in 1896. They are: Australia, Great Britain, France, Greece, and Switzerland.

SOMETHING NEW

When the Olympic Games visit Sydney in the year 2000, they will include a new sailing event. This is the exciting high-performance double-handed dinghy called the 49-er. (You can find out more about it on pages 8-9.)

Sailing in a 49-er

OLYMPICS FACT FILE

- *The Olympic Games were first held in Olympia, Greece, about 3,000 years ago. They took place every four years until they were abolished in A. D. 393.*
- *A Frenchman named Pierre de Coubertin (1863–1937) revived the Games, and the first modern Olympics were held in Athens in 1896.*
- *The modern Games have been held every four years since 1896, except in 1916, 1940, and 1944, because of war. Special 10th-anniversary Games took place in 1906.*
- *The symbol of the Olympic Games is five interlocking colored rings. Together, they represent the five different continents from which athletes come to compete.*

WHAT A RECORD!

The most successful competitor in any water sport was the Danish single-handed yachtsman Paul Elvström. In 1960, he became the first person in Olympic history to win four gold medals in a row in the same event. His Olympic career lasted for 40 years, and he attended eight Games from 1948 to 1988—another record!

Paul Elvström

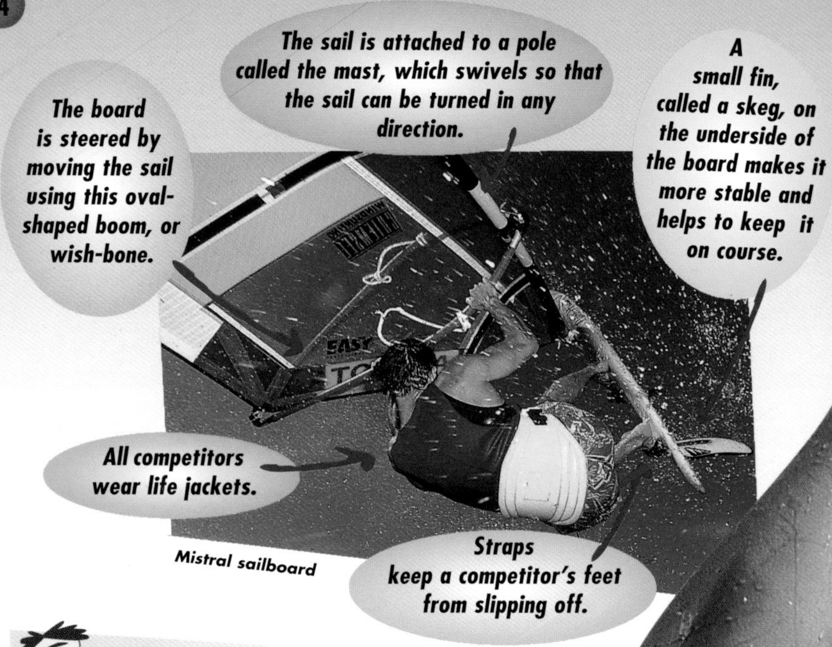
The sail is attached to a pole called the mast, which swivels so that the sail can be turned in any direction.
The board is steered by moving the sail using this oval-shaped boom, or wish-bone.
A small fin, called a skeg, on the underside of the board makes it more stable and helps to keep it on course.
EASY
All competitors wear life jackets.
Straps keep a competitor's feet from slipping off.

Mistral sailboard

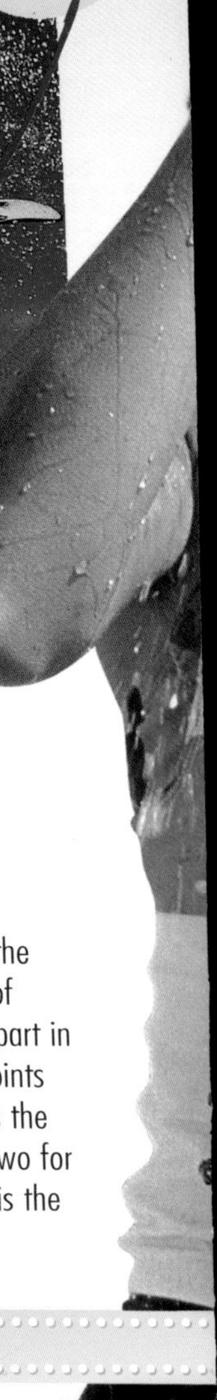

DID YOU KNOW?

- The mistral is the only event in which competitors are not penalized for bumping into the buoys.
- Sailboarders usually compete barefoot because this improves their grip on the board.
- Sailboard competitors use the transparent window in the sail to see where they are going.

BUOY OH BOY!

As in other sailing events, competitors in the mistral have to race around a course marked with floating markers called buoys (BOO-ees). Each race takes about an hour to complete.

MAKING YOUR POINT

Like most Olympic sailing competitions, the mistral events are decided by a series of 11 fleet races, and every competitor takes part in all the races. Competitors are awarded points according to the order in which they cross the finish line—one point for coming in first, two for coming in second, and so on. The winner is the person with the lowest score.

REIGNING OLYMPIC CHAMPIONS: **Men**: Nikolaos Kaklamanakis (GRE)

MISTRAL

Stick a sail on a surfboard and what do you get? The answer is a sailboard—although it goes by many other names!

Lee Lai-shan

WHAT'S IN A NAME?

Board sailing, surfboarding, windgliding, sailboarding, and windsurfing are all different names for the Olympic event known as the mistral!

Competitors need strong arms, agility, and a superb sense of balance to become a mistral champion like Lee Lai-shan (HKG).

SUPER STATS

The greatest speed ever achieved on a sailboard is 51 mph (83 km/h). That's 10 times quicker than the fastest Olympic swimmer!

Women: Lee Lai-shan (HKG)

SINGLE-HANDED DINGHIES

Each boat in the single-handed dinghy events is sailed by one person alone.

SAILING COURSE

To test the sailors' skills, the Olympic sailing courses are designed so that the wind blows in different directions in different parts of the course.

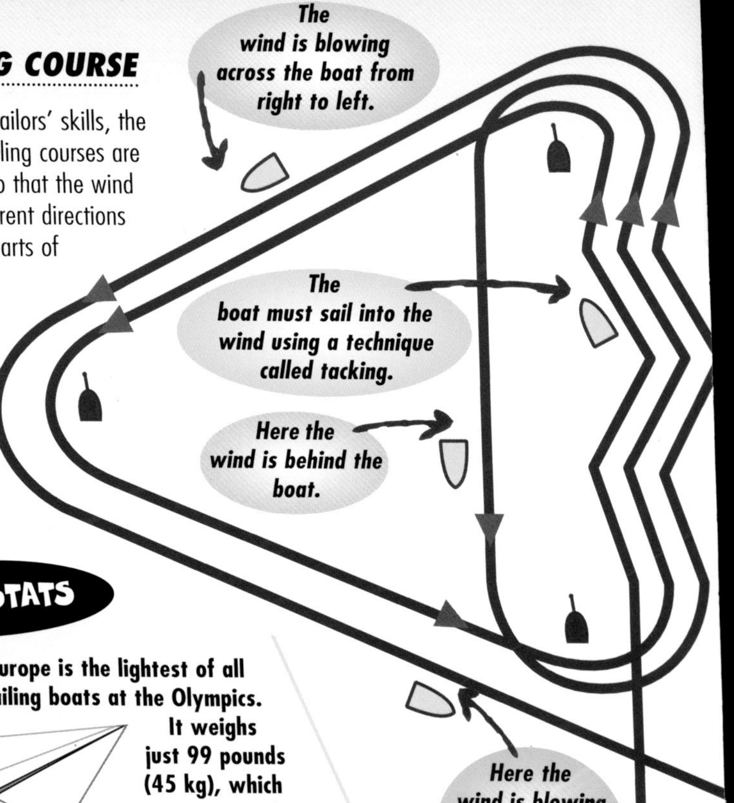

The wind is blowing across the boat from right to left.
The boat must sail into the wind using a technique called tacking.
Here the wind is behind the boat.
Here the wind is blowing across the boat from left to right.
STARTI
LINE

SUPER STATS

The Europe is the lightest of all the sailing boats at the Olympics. It weighs just 99 pounds (45 kg), which means it weighs less than the competitor inside it!

REIGNING OLYMPIC CHAMPIONS: Finn: Mateusz Kusznierewicz (POL)

Ben Ainslie

TAKE A HIKE

A strong wind can cause a boat to capsize. To prevent this, competitors use a technique called hiking out. They lean out over the water, using their own body weight to balance the force of the wind and keep their boats upright. Here Ben Ainslie (GBR), the 1996 laser silver medalist, shows how it's done.

FINN, EUROPE, & LASER

There will be three single-handed dinghy events at the Sydney Olympics: finn (the men's event), Europe (the women's event), and laser. The laser is an open event, in which both men and women can compete.

TACKLING TACKING

The hardest part of the course is the stretch that sails into the wind, so during that part, yachters use a technique called tacking. They sail forward in a zig-zag path. Setting the sails at exactly the right angle and judging when to change course requires great skill.

DID YOU KNOW?

Olympic events involving boats with sails used to be called yachting but for the Sydney Games, the sport has been officially renamed sailing.

Single-handed dinghies are also called monotypes.

At the 1988 Games, Lawrence Lemieux (CAN) was awarded a special medal for rescuing another yachtsman who was swept out to sea after capsizing.

Europe: Kristine Roug (DEN), **Laser**: Robert Scheidt (BRA)

This sail is called the mainsail or mainsheet.

TRAPEZE ACT

On a 470, one crew member (the helmsman) steers the boat while the other hikes out. By attaching a wire (known as a trapeze) to the harness, the helmsman is able to lean right out over the water. Here, Yevhen Braslavets and Ihor Matviyenko (UKR), the reigning men's 470 champions, in action.

DID YOU KNOW?

- *At the Olympics, all the crew members in a boat must be of the same nationality.*
- *The 470 was invented in 1963 and immediately became one of the most popular small sailing boats.*
- *Like most other sailing events, the 49-er class is decided by a series of fleet races. Unlike the others, there are 16 races.*

THE 470 & 49-ER

In the 470 class, men and women compete in separate events but the new 49-er competition is an open event.

The 49-er class dinghies have a double trapeze. This means that both crew members can hike out together and set the sails to catch more of the wind, and so increase their speed.

49-er with spinnaker

REIGNING OLYMPIC CHAMPIONS: Men's 470: Yevhen Braslavets and Ihor Matviyenko (UKR)

DOUBLE-HANDED DINGHIES

A new double-handed event called the 49-er will make its Olympic debut in Sydney.

This sail, called a spinnaker, is used for extra speed when the wind is behind the boat.

IN A SPIN

Sailors who break one of the rules of sailing are penalized. This involves sailing around in a circle either once or twice, depending on the boat and the rule broken. If a penalty lap is not performed properly, the sailor may be disqualified.

The small sail in front of the mainsail is called the jib.

ANIMAL OLYMPIANS

With a top speed of around 42 mph (68 km/h), the 49-er may be the fastest boat at the Games but it's not as fast as the bluefin tuna, which can travel at 46.5 mph (75 km/h).

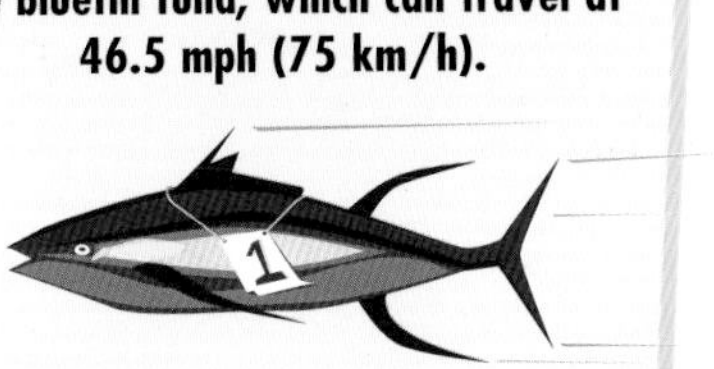

Women's 470: Theresa Zabell and Begona Via Dufresne (ESP) **49-er**: This will be held for the first time at Sydney.

THE STAR

The star is another double-handed sailing event, but unlike the double-handed dinghy competitions, the boats in this category have fixed keels.

STARTER'S SIGNALS

Six minutes before the start of each race, officials in a boat stationed next to the starting line give a signal by firing a cannon or sounding a loud blast of a horn. One minute later, another signal is given. A third signal is given one minute before the start of the race. The fourth means the race has started.

LEARN THE LINGO

Beat: part of the course that forces the crew to luff

Knot: the speed of boats is often measured in knots. 1 knot equals 1.1 mph (1.85 km/h)

Luff: to sail into the wind

Inspecting the keel

JUMPING THE GUN!

Competitors aim to cross the line a split second after the fourth signal has been given. A boat that crosses the line before this signal must sail around in a circle back behind the starting line and start again.

Torben Grael and Marcelo Ferreira, Atlanta 1996

The star is an open event. At the 1996 Games, it was won by Torben Grael and Marcelo Ferreira (BRA).

KNOW YOUR BOAT

Boom: holds the bottom of the mainsail so that it catches the wind
Bow: the front of a boat
Hull: main body of the boat
Keel: keeps the boat steady
Mast: holds the sails up
Rudder: used to steer the boat
Stern: the back of a boat
Tiller: controls the rudder

The fin on the bottom of a boat is called the keel. It helps the boat to sail in a straight line and stay upright. The crew on a dinghy can raise or lower its keel, but the bigger boats in the star class have fixed keels that cannot be adjusted.

DID YOU KNOW?

- *The first star class boat was built in 1911.*
- *The star event was first held at the Olympics in 1932, but the oldest sailing event at the Games is the finn, which was introduced in 1924.*
- *Between 1948 and 1988, sailor Durward Knowles (GBR/BAH) competed in a record-eight Olympic Games.*

SILVER: Sweden **BRONZE:** Australia

DID YOU KNOW?

The boats used in the soling competition are the largest at the Games, but in 1900 there was a race for boats weighing more than 20 tons!

There are more than 3,000 different classes of sailing boat, but only nine are Olympic events.

Soling has been part of every Olympic sailing competition since 1972.

CHAMPION TACTICS!

To win a match race, competitors try to maneuver their boats so that they force their opponents to make a mistake and break one of the rules. Making the other boat incur penalties slows it down, giving the opposing crew time to race into the lead!

MUSCLE MEN

The reigning Olympic soling champions are Jochen Schumann, Thomas Flach, and Bernd Jaekel (GER). Like the star, soling is an open event. However, competitors in both the star and the soling classes are almost always men because handling these large boats requires a great deal of muscle.

Jochen Schumann, Thomas Flach, Bernd Jaekel, Atlanta 1996

1996 OLYMPIC MEDALISTS: **GOLD:** Germany

Soling final, Russia vs. Germany, Atlanta 1996

SOLING

Unlike all the other sailing events at the Games, competitors in the soling class sail in races known as match races.

ONE-ON-ONE

The first round of the soling event is decided by a fleet race but the rest of the competition is made up of match races. Unlike a fleet race, which involves all the competitors, a match race is a head-to-head competition between two boats on a much shorter course.

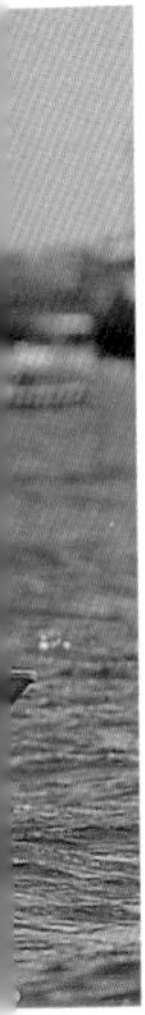

AYE AYE SKIPPER

Boats with more than one person in them always have a skipper. It's the skipper's job to decide on tactics and to tell the other members of the crew what to do and when to do it. Good communication and discipline onboard are the key to success!

SUPER STATS

The United States and Norway have each won 16 gold medals in the sailing events—more than any other nation! Next is Great Britain with 14 medals, then France with 12.

SILVER: Russia **BRONZE:** United States

TORNADO

The event for catamarans at the Olympics is called the tornado—so prepare to be blown away!

COOL CATS

Catamarans have two hulls, one on either side of the deck. They are much lighter than other similarly sized boats, enabling them to sail across the water extremely quickly. With a good wind behind them, they can reach a top speed of about 30 mph (50 km/h).

ANIMAL OLYMPIANS

You wouldn't get far in a catamaran if you were being chased by a hungry tiger shark! These fearsome fish can swim faster than even the fastest catamarans. And if there was a gold medal for eating people, they might win that, too!

HARBOR VIEW

Most of the different sailing events at the 2000 Games will take place inside Sydney Harbour. This means that the competitors will get a good view of two of Australia's most famous landmarks: the Sydney Harbour Bridge and the Sydney Opera House.

1996 OLYMPIC MEDALISTS: **GOLD**: Spain

Gloves help in gripping the slippery ropes.
Both crew members wear life jackets, just in case they fall overboard!
Some yachtsmen wear a wet suit to help them keep warm, but others don't bother!
Lightweight rubber shoes with ribbed soles stop the sailors from slipping.

Fernando Leon and Jose Luis Ballester (ESP), Atlanta 1996

Sydney Harbour

FATHER & DAUGHTER

The great Danish yachtsman Paul Elvström (see page 3) took part in the Olympics for the first time in 1948. His last Olympic race was in 1988 when he sailed in the tornado event. His partner in the race was his daughter, Trine.

DID YOU KNOW?

- *The design of the catamaran is based on an ancient type of boat invented thousands of years ago in Asia.*
- *The course used in the tornado class is designed so that the race will last about 90 minutes.*
- *Catamarans aren't the only kind of boat with more than one hull. There's also a three-hull boat called a trimaran.*

SILVER: Australia **BRONZE:** Brazil

Only six lanes are used in each race.

The water on the course cannot be less than 11 feet (3.5 meters) deep.

DID YOU KNOW?

Rowing events at the Olympic Games used to be held on rivers.

After winning the men's individual sculls at the 1956 Games, Vyacheslav Ivanov (URS) threw his gold medal up into the air. It landed in Lake Wendouree and was lost forever!

Even though rowing events are held on still-water courses, the water and weather conditions still vary too much for official world or Olympic records.

The course is divided into nine lanes, separated by colored buoys.

THE COURSE

Sculling races, like all the other rowing events, are 1.24 miles (2,000 meters) long and take place on a perfectly straight, artificial course, which is sheltered from the wind. Its banks are sloped and covered with gravel to help absorb waves, keeping the surface of the water flat and still.

REIGNING OLYMPIC CHAMPIONS: **MEN**: **Single sculls:** Xeno Mueller (SUI) **Double sculls:** Davide Tizzano and Agostino Abbagnale (ITA
Lightweight double sculls: Michael Gier and Markus Gier (SUI) **Quadruple sculls:** Germany

Men's lightweight double sculls race

SCULLING

Each competitor has two oars, one in each hand, for the sculling events.

Katrin Rutschow

Katrin Rutschow (GER) won a gold at the 1996 Games in the women's quad (4-person) sculls event.

Rowers wear lightweight shorts and vests made out of stretchy materials.

In rowing, boats travel backward.

The color of the buoys indicates the distance to the finish line.

WINNING QUALITIES

Rowing requires powerful arm, chest, leg, and stomach muscles. Maintaining a steady pace with the oars is crucial and requires precise timing, which is why top rowers, such as Katrin Rutschow (GER), also need a superb sense of natural rhythm.

WOMEN: **Single sculls:** Yekaterina Khodotovich (BLR) **Double sculls:** Marnie McBean and Kathleen Heddle (CAN) **Lightweight double sculls:** Constantina Burcica and Camelia Macoviciuc (ROM) / **Quadruple sculls:** Germany

SWEEP OAR (COXED)

Make way for the mighty Eights, the largest and fastest rowing boats at the Games.

The cox is the only person in the boat who can see where to go!

WHY 8 = 9!

The Eights are sweep oar rowing events. Unlike sculling races, each rower has only one oar, not two. The event is called Eights because the boats are rowed by eight people, although there are actually nine people aboard each boat! The extra crew member is the coxswain ("cox" for short).

SUPER STATS

The boats used in the Eights are 56 feet (17 meters) long. That's just over twice the length of a single scull boat!

REIGNING OLYMPIC CHAMPIONS: **Men's Eights:** Netherlands

IN THE DRIVING SEAT

The cox's job is to keep the other members of the team rowing in a smooth, steady rhythm and to decide how fast they should row. Coxes are also responsible for steering the boat and making it go in a straight line.

Lightweight Eights (GBR)

GOLDEN BOY

At the Games in 1900 (before minimum weight limits were introduced), one team decided that its cox was too heavy. Team members asked a young boy in the crowd to take his place! The team and its new cox won the final, and the boy (name unknown and thought to be younger than 10 years old) was presented with a gold medal.

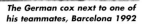

The German cox next to one of his teammates, Barcelona 1992

LIGHT WORK

Although a light cox is best, there are minimum weight limits: 121 pounds (55 kg) in the men's event and 110 pounds (50 kg) in the women's. If the cox weighs less than the limit, extra weight is added to the boat to make up the difference.

DID YOU KNOW?

- *The cox in Olympic races must be the same sex as the rest of the crew.*
- *A crew can continue racing if one of the rowers falls out of the boat but not if the cox falls out!*
- *The youngest cox whose age and name are known for certain was 12-year-old Noël Vandernotte (FRA), who won two gold medals in 1936.*

Steven Redgrave with his British teammates Pinsent, Cracknell, and Coope

DID YOU KNOW?

- *Competitors in coxless boats steer using a rudder that's controlled by pedals.*
- *Competitors in the lightweight event must weigh less than 160 pounds (72.5 kg).*
- *In 1980 and 1992, two pairs of twins raced against each other in the final of the coxless pairs!*

OARSOME!

Seven-time world champion, Steven Redgrave (GBR), will be competing for his fifth gold medal at the Sydney Games.

The competitors' shoes are attached to a plate on the bottom of the boat.

The seats inside the boat are mounted on rails to allow the rowers to slide forward and backward while they row and increase the power of each stroke.

REIGNING OLYMPIC CHAMPIONS: MEN: Coxless pair: Steven Redgrave and Matthew Pinsent (GBR), **Coxless four:** Australia

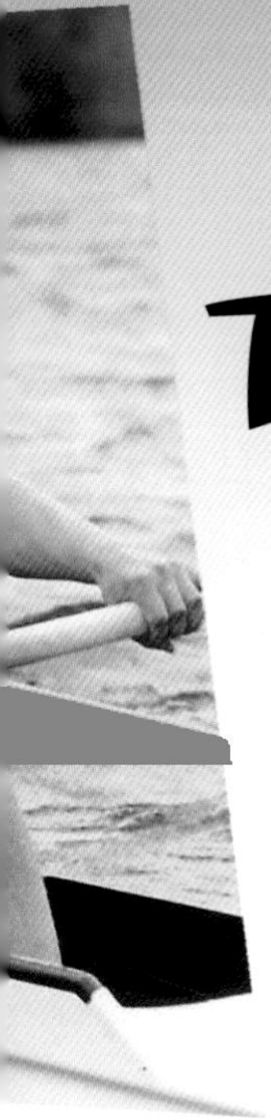

SWEEP OAR (COXLESS)

There are four other sweep oar rowing races at the Olympics, but there is no room for a cox in these events.

UNDER STARTER'S ORDERS

At the start of each race, the boats are held in position by a device called a boot. When the crews are ready, an official shouts "Two minutes" and reads out the names of all the competitors taking part. If the light controlled by the judges has turned white, the official shouts "Attention!" and then presses a button that beeps loudly. At that instant, the boot automatically releases the boats.

THE EVENTS

The coxless pairs is a race with one event for men and another for women, plus the men-only events of the coxless four and the lightweight coxless four.

Boats are usually made of wood.
The outrigger supports the weight of the oar, helping the boat to go faster.

Rowing boat

LEARN THE LINGO

Bow: **the name also given to the rower who sits at the front**

Shell: **another name for a racing boat**

Stroke: **the name given to the person who sits at the back of the boat**

Lightweight coxless four: Denmark **WOMEN**: **Coxless pair:** Megan Still and Kate Slatter (AUS)

CANOE

Unlike a rowing boat, the paddle that powers a canoe must not be fixed to the boat in any way.

ANCIENT ORIGINS

The Native Americans made canoes from hollowed-out tree trunks, which they knelt in to paddle. Modern canoes are based on this design, but are much more streamlined than the traditional-style canoe shown below.

Paddles are not fixed to the boat and are used on either side.

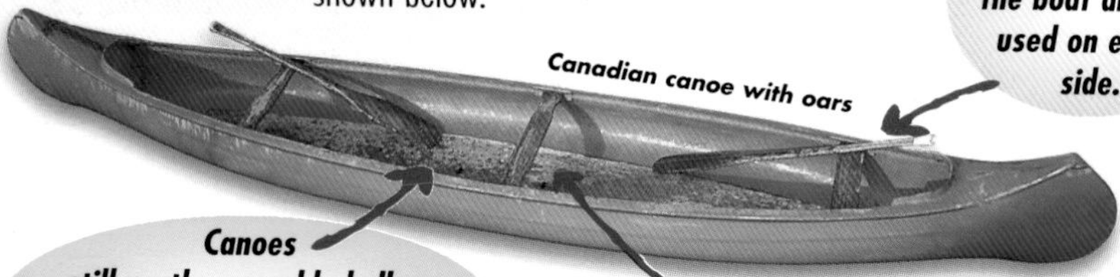

Canoes still partly resemble hollow tree trunks in shape but are made of fiberglass.

Canoeists kneel inside the canoe so there's no need for seats.

PADDLE POWER

The paddles used by canoeists have a handle to grip at one end and a flat blade for pushing through the water at the other. The paddles are also used to steer. For example, paddling hard on one side makes the canoe turn toward the other side.

SUPER STATS

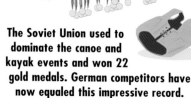

The Soviet Union used to dominate the canoe and kayak events and won 22 gold medals. German competitors have now equaled this impressive record. Meanwhile, Sweden has notched 12 victories, and Hungary has 9.

WHO CAN'T CANOE?

Sprint races take place over 547 yards (500 meters) and 1,094 yards (1,000 meters), and there are events for one-man and two-man canoes. But there are no canoeing events for women.

REIGNING OLYMPIC CHAMPIONS: **Canoe single 500:** Martin Doktor (CZE), **Canoe single 1000:** Martin Doktor (CZE)

Martin Doktor, Atlanta 1996

DOING THE DOUBLE

The sprint events are a simple headlong dash to the finish line. The winner is the first to cross the line—as long as the boat is the right way up! Both the individual sprints at the 1996 Olympics were won by Martin Doktor (CZE).

DID YOU KNOW?

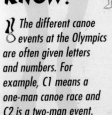

The different canoe events at the Olympics are often given letters and numbers. For example, C1 means a one-man canoe race and C2 is a two-man event.

Canoeists are forbidden to ride on the wash (waves) created by another competitor's canoe in front of them.

Canoes are only allowed to have a tiny keel that can't stick out more than 1.2 inches (3 cm) from the hull.

Canoe double 500: Gyorgy Kolonios and Csaba Horvath (HUN) **Canoe double 1000**: Andreas Dittmer and Gunar Kirchbach (GER)

KAYAK

When is a canoe not a canoe? When it's a kayak!

TRADITIONAL DESIGN

Modern kayaks, like canoes, are also based on a traditional type of boat. Kayaks were invented by the Inuit people who live in the Arctic. They would stretch sealskins over frames made out of whalebone and then rub blubber (fat from seals and whales) all over the finished boats to make them watertight.

GOLDEN GIRLS

The women's sprint races are 500 meters long. There are 500-meter and 1,000-meter races for men. As in the canoe events, there are races for both one and two-person kayaks, known as K1 and K2 for short.

Antonio Rossi

SPOT THE DIFFERENCE

Competitors in kayaks sit down to paddle, unlike Olympic canoeists who kneel. Another difference is that sprint kayaks have a rudder. The paddles are different too. Kayak paddles are longer and have a blade at each end.

SPLIT-SECOND VICTORY

After the 1,000-meter kayak sprint at the 1988 Games, the judges deliberated for more than 10 minutes before announcing that Greg Barton (USA) had crossed the finish line first—just 0.005 seconds ahead of Grant Davies (AUS)!

REIGNING OLYMPIC CHAMPIONS: **MEN**: **Kayak single 500**: Antonio Rossi (ITA) **Kayak single 1000**: Knut Holmann (NOR) **Kayak double 500**: Kay Bluhm and Torsten Gutsche (GER) **Kayak double 1000**: Antonio Rossi and Daniele Scarpa (ITA)

DID YOU KNOW?

- Between 1948 and 1960, Gert Fredriksson (SWE) won six gold medals, a silver, and a bronze in Olympic kayak events.
- At the Games in 1936, there were separate events for folding kayaks, which could be dismantled and carried around in bags.
- Kayaks were introduced into Europe 150 years ago by an English lawyer named John MacGregor.

Antonio Rossi (ITA) won the gold medal at the 1996 Games in the men's K1 500-meter single and K2 1,000-meter races.

Greg Barton

SUPER STATS

By holding on to each other's paddles, several people join their kayaks together to form a raft. The largest raft ever formed in this way was made up of 648 different kayaks.

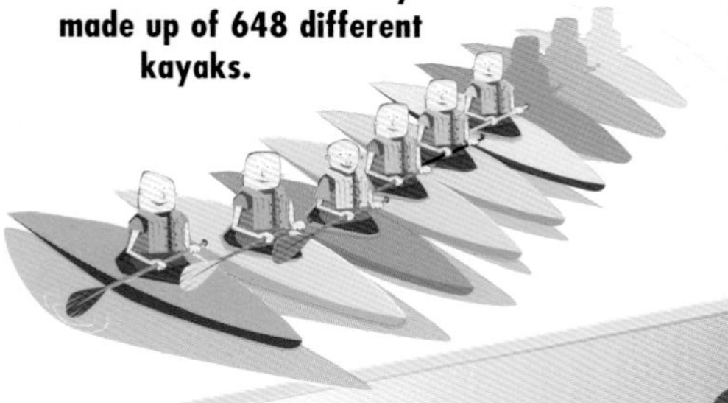

WOMEN: **Kayak single 500**: Rita Koban (HUN) **Kayak double 500**: Agneta Andersson and Susanne Gunnarsson (SWE)
The women's kayak single and double 1000 events were not held at the 1996 Games.

KAYAK: FOURS

When traveling at full speed, competitors in the four-person kayak can paddle up to 130 strokes a minute. That's more than two strokes every second!

PULLING TOGETHER

This picture was taken during the women's fours event at the 1996 Olympics. Look closely and you will see how every member of each team is holding her paddle in almost exactly the same position. In kayak and canoe events, as in rowing, precise rhythm and timing are the keys to success.

SUPER STATS

A four-person kayak has a top speed of more than 12 mph (20 km/h). That's fast enough to pull someone along on water skis!

Look at the paddle. See how the two blades at each end are set at different angles? This means that as one blade is being pulled flat-side-on through the water, the other is cutting through the air thin-side-on.

Women's kayak fours, Atlanta 1996

Flat water canoe, Atlanta 1996

CLEAN SWEEP

At the 1996 Games in Atlanta, the men's and women's K4 events were both won by the teams from Germany. It was the first time one nation had won both events at the same Games.

DID YOU KNOW?

The four-person kayak made its Olympic debut in 1964.

Women took part in the event for the first time in 1984.

The men's K4 race is twice as long as the women's event. Men race 1,000 meters, and women compete for 500 meters.

READY, STEADY, GO

Kayak races are started by an official stationed in a small hut alongside the starting line. When all the competitors are ready, the starter shouts "Attention, please," then fires a starting pistol. A competitor who jumps the gun twice and makes two false starts is disqualified..

NO PENALTIES

Canoeists in the slalom events try to go around the course as quickly as possible, avoiding penalties. A 2-second penalty is added to their final time if they (or their paddle or canoe) touch one of the gate poles. Missing a gate incurs a massive 50-second penalty!

Down-stream gates have green-and-white poles.

DID YOU KNOW?

- *In 1992, 12-time world champion Jon Lugbill (USA) finished the course in the fastest time but missed out on a medal because his life jacket touched a pole on the second from last gate!*
- *Competitors start the course at 180-second intervals.*
- *Slalom events in canoes, like the sprint events, are for men only.*

Michal Martikan (SVK) was only 17 when he won the gold medal in the individual slalom event at the 1996 Games.

Michal Martikan (SVK), Men's C1 slalom, Atlanta 1996

SLALOM CANOES

The boats used in slalom events are wider and shorter than the ones used in sprint races, and the top of a slalom canoe is covered to prevent water coming in over the sides. Canoeists paddle while kneeling, using a paddle with only one blade.

REIGNING OLYMPIC CHAMPIONS: **Canoe singles:** Michal Martikan (SVK)

Canoe slalom course

Up-stream gates have red-and-white poles.

CANOE: SLALOM

The canoeists in sprint events face water that is flat and still, but in the slalom events, canoeists battle a torrent!

SPLASHING OUT

Water rushes down the 300-meter long slalom course, creating swirling whirlpools and powerful currents. Along the course are 25 gates, which competitors must pass though without touching. Six of the gates must be negotiated upstream.

IT'S A FAKE!

The U-shaped slalom course used at the Games in Sydney looks like a natural mountain river, but it's completely artificial!

SUPER STATS

The top of the slalom course at Sydney is more than 5.5 yards (5 meters) higher than the bottom. That's higher than a double-decker bus!

Canoe doubles: Frank Adisson and Wilfrid Forgues (FRA)

KAYAK: SLALOM

Unlike sprint kayaks, the boats used in slalom events must not have rudders. Instead, the competitors must steer by paddling.

Slalom competitors must wear safety helmets.

Kayak slalom course

KEEPING A WATCHFUL EYE

Up to three judges watch each gate on the course to see if the competitors touch them as they go through. All decisions are made according to what the judges see with the naked eye.

SUPER STATS

In 1987, a British canoeist performed 1,000 Eskimo rolls in just 34 minutes, setting a world record!

ROLL OVER

The power of the water tumbling down the course is often enough to capsize the boats and turn them upside down. But competitors just stay inside their canoe and paddle underwater to turn the right way up again. This technique is known as an Eskimo roll.

REIGNING OLYMPIC CHAMPIONS: **Men's kayak singles**: Oliver Fix (GER)

There are events for both men and women in the kayak slalom.
The reigning Olympic women's champion is Stepanka Hilgertova (CZE).
Life jackets are worn in all slalom events.
Slalom competitors wear a spray skirt around their middle. This stretches across the top of the cockpit and keeps water out.
The competitor sits in a hole called the cockpit.
Atlanta 1996

Stepanka Hilgertova, Atlanta 1996

DID YOU KNOW?

- *Before the 1972 Olympics, the East German team spent months practicing on an exact replica of the artificial river that had been built for the Games. They went on to win all of the gold medals!*
- *The layout of the gates is redesigned for the final of each event.*
- *Competitors from more than 30 different countries will take part in the slalom events at the Games.*

PUMP IT UP

Because Sydney's slalom course is not a natural flowing river, six powerful pumps are needed to push the water at the bottom of the course back up to the top again. These pumps will have to work really hard as water cascades down the course at a rate of 14 tons every second!

Women's kayak singles: Stepanka Hilgertova (CZE)

INDEX

Acknowledgments
We would like to thank Ian Hodge, Rosalind Beckman, and Elizabeth Wiggans for their assistance. Cartoons by John Alston.

Printed in Hong Kong.
First published in Great Britain by ticktock Publishing Ltd., The Offices in the Square, Hadlow, Tonbridge, Kent TN11 0DD, Great Britain.
Picture Credits: Allsport: IFC, OFC, 3br, 4t, 4–5 (main pic), 7tr, 8tl, 11tr, 12–13b, 14–15b, 18–19c, 19bl, 20–21 (main pic), 25t, 26–27 (main pic), 27tr, 28–29 (main pic), 30t; Empics: 16–17 (main pic), 17r, 22–23 (main pic), 24–25 (main pic), 28br, 30–31 (main pic); Kos Picture Source: 2–3 (main pic), 8–9 (main pic), 12–13t, 14–15t, 20–21b; PPL: 10–11 (main pic), 22t.
Picture research by Image Select.
Library of Congress Cataloging-in-Publication Data
Page, Jason.
On the water : rowing, yachting, canoeing, and lots, lots more / by Jason Page.
p. cm. -- (Zeke's Olympic pocket guide)
Includes index.
Summary: Describes the sailing, rowing, and canoeing events of the Olympic Games and previews the athletic competition at the 2000 Summer Olympics in Sydney, Australia.
ISBN 0-8225-5051-2 (pbk. : alk. paper)
1. Aquatic sports--Juvenile literature. 2. Olympics--Juvenile literature. [1. Aquatic sports. 2. Olympics.] I. Title. II. Series.
GV770.5 .P35 2000
797.1--dc21
00-008151